D1271248

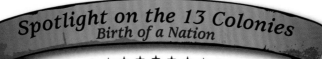

Spotlight on the 13 Colonies
Birth of a Nation

★ ★ ★ ★ ★ ★ ★ ★ ★ ★ ★ ★

THE COLONY OF
NORTH
CAROLINA

Joyce Jeffries

PowerKiDS press™

NEW YORK

St. John's School
Lower Library
Houston, TX

Published in 2016 by The Rosen Publishing Group, Inc.
29 East 21st Street, New York, NY 10010

Copyright © 2016 by The Rosen Publishing Group, Inc.

All rights reserved. No part of this book may be reproduced in any form without permission in writing from the publisher, except by a reviewer.

Editor: Katie Kawa
Book Design: Andrea Davison-Bartolotta

Photo Credits: Cover North Wind Picture Archives; p. 4 National Portrait Gallery/Wikimedia Commons; p. 5 (main) DEA/G. DAGLI ORTI/Getty Images; p. 5 (inset) Dennis K. Johnson/Getty Images; p. 6 IgorSokol/ Wikimedia Commons; p. 7 Egbert van Heemskerk the Elder/Getty Images; pp. 8–9 BotMultichillT/Wikimedia Commons; pp. 10–11 Panoramic Images/Getty Images; p. 11 (inset) Print Collector/Getty Images; pp. 12–13 Guy J. Sagi/Shutterstock.com; p. 13 (inset) Jeff Willhelm/Charlotte Observer/Getty Images; pp. 14–15 MPI/ Stringer/Getty Images; p. 16 OttawaAC/Wikimedia Commons; p. 17 Courtesy of Library of Congress; p. 19 Zack Frank/Shutterstock.com; p. 21 DoxaDigital/iStock/Thinkstock; p. 22 VectorPic/Shutterstock.com.

Library of Congress Cataloging-in-Publication Data

Jeffries, Joyce.
The colony of North Carolina / by Joyce Jeffries.
p. cm. — (Spotlight on the 13 colonies: Birth of a nation)
Includes index.
ISBN 978-1-4994-0554-5 (pbk.)
ISBN 978-1-4994-0556-9 (6 pack)
ISBN 978-1-4994-0558-3 (library binding)
1. North Carolina — History — Colonial period, ca. 1600 - 1775 — Juvenile literature. 2. North Carolina — History — 1775 - 1865 — Juvenile literature. I. Jeffries, Joyce. II. Title.
F257.J44 2016
975.6/02 —d23

Manufactured in the United States of America

CPSIA Compliance Information: Batch #WS15PK: For further information contact Rosen Publishing, New York, New York at 1-800-237-9932.

Contents

A Lost Colony. 4

A Permanent Settlement 6

Culpeper's Rebellion 8

Life in the New Colony. 10

Unrest in the West 12

War and Taxes 14

Tea Parties 16

Fighting the British 18

A Call to Independence 20

Statehood for North Carolina 22

Glossary 23

Index. 24

Primary Source List. 24

Websites 24

A Lost Colony

Native Americans lived in North Carolina long before it became a colony. Tribes such as the Tuscarora, Catawba, and Cherokee lived in the area that would become North Carolina before the earliest European explorers arrived in the 1500s.

Italian explorer Giovanni da Verrazano was the first European to reach North Carolina. He sailed to the mouth of the Cape Fear River in 1524. The first English settlers to reach present-day North Carolina were a group sent by Sir Walter Raleigh in 1585. Queen Elizabeth I granted Raleigh land in North Carolina one year before the settlers arrived. They established a colony on Roanoke Island, which is off North Carolina's coast. However, they had difficulty finding enough food, so they returned to England.

In 1587, a second group of settlers came to Roanoke Island. Three years later, supply ships from England reached the colony, but found no settlers left on the island. The Roanoke colony became known as the "Lost Colony," and the mystery of what happened has never been solved.

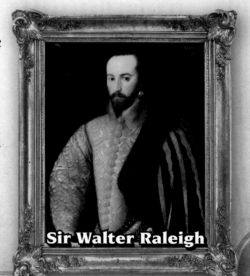

Sir Walter Raleigh

SECOTAN

Pasquenoke

Dasamonquepeuc

Roanoke

Trinety harbor

Hatorasck

1896

Roanoke Island can be seen off the coast in this map, which was meant to show the land given to Sir Walter Raleigh. Today, a stone marker on Roanoke Island serves as a reminder of the Lost Colony.

A Permanent Settlement

After the failure of the Lost Colony, many years passed before people began **permanently** settling in North Carolina. In the 1650s, settlers from Virginia began moving into areas in North Carolina. However, it wasn't until 1663 that Carolina—which included modern-day North Carolina, South Carolina, and Georgia—became an official colony. That year, King Charles II of England made Carolina a proprietary—or privately owned—colony and granted its land to eight men.

King Charles II

Settlers in Carolina had religious freedom, so many came to the colony to escape religious **persecution**. Quakers came to Carolina and became an important part of both religious and political life in the colony. The Quakers, who are also known as the Society of Friends, believe in the equality of all people, so they have no **clergy**. They also don't believe in violence. Quakers were persecuted by the Church of England because of their beliefs. Quakers in Carolina were able to practice their beliefs freely.

In making Carolina a proprietary colony, King Charles II gave control to the eight men who owned it. By allowing religious freedom, these men opened the colony to people such as the Quakers, who held services like the one shown here throughout North Carolina.

7

Culpeper's Rebellion

In 1669, the Fundamental Constitutions of Carolina set up a government for the entire colony. However, the settlers didn't always agree with the way the colony was governed. This was especially true in the area that would become North Carolina.

In 1677, colonists in the Albemarle section of Carolina staged an uprising against their **deputy** governor, Thomas Miller. The colonists were angry because of the Carolina government's **enforcement** of high British taxes. A group led by John Culpeper and George Durant **imprisoned** Miller and took over the government of the northern part of Carolina. This uprising was known as Culpeper's Rebellion. This new government was in power for two years. Then, in 1679, the owners of the colony, who were also called the proprietors, stepped in and restored the proprietary government.

That same year, Miller returned to England and tried to send Culpeper to jail. However, he was unsuccessful, and Culpeper wasn't punished for his acts of rebellion.

This map from 1715 shows the colonies of Carolina, Virginia, Maryland, and New Jersey. Albemarle County, which was the site of Culpeper's Rebellion, can be seen near the top of the area of the map marked "Carolina."

Life in the New Colony

North Carolina and South Carolina were treated as separate areas even before the colonies were officially split in 1712. Although one governor was in charge of the whole colony of Carolina and ruled from Charles Town (now called Charleston, South Carolina), a deputy governor oversaw the area that would become North Carolina.

In 1705, North Carolina's first official town, Bath, was founded. Five years later, settlers from Switzerland and Germany, under the leadership of Christoph von Graffenried, established a town on the Neuse and the Trent Rivers. This town, named New Bern, is the second-oldest town in North Carolina. It officially became a city in 1723 and became the capital of the colony.

Tryon Palace, shown here, was where the royal governor lived in New Bern.

Life in the new colony of North Carolina wasn't easy. The settlers often feared for their safety. Colonists fought with members of the Tuscarora tribe in the Tuscarora War, which lasted from 1711 to 1713. The colonists also faced attacks by pirates. Blackbeard was a feared pirate who attacked ships along the coast of North Carolina.

members of the Tuscarora tribe

Unrest in the West

North Carolina came under the direct rule of the king of England when it became a royal colony in 1729. During its time as a royal colony, North Carolina grew in population and wealth. In 1735, its borders with South Carolina were set, although there continued to be **disputes** over those borders for many years.

Not all areas of North Carolina felt they were sharing in the colony's growth. Colonists in the western part of North Carolina grew angry with those in the eastern part. The government of North Carolina was centered in the eastern part of the colony, and some western colonists felt they weren't being fairly represented in the colonial government.

These angry colonists formed a group called the Regulators. They refused to pay taxes and tried to rise up against the government. This uprising was known as the War of Regulation. Governor William Tryon squashed their rebellion during the Battle of Alamance on May 16, 1771.

rice

North Carolina's colonial economy grew rapidly thanks to its two biggest crops: tobacco and rice.

tobacco

War and Taxes

The British and the French fought for control over North America in the French and Indian War, which lasted from 1754 to 1763. The war got its name from the fact that both the British and the French were aided by Native American **allies**. The British won the war, but it cost a lot of money. To pay for the cost of the war, Britain decided to tax the colonies. These taxes were also meant to help pay for the cost of keeping the peace between colonists and Native Americans after the war.

Britain passed the Stamp Act in 1765. This called for a tax on many different kinds of paper goods and dice in the colonies. Groups were formed in all the colonies, including North Carolina, to protest the Stamp Act and other taxes. These groups were called the Sons of Liberty. Members of these groups believed it was wrong to tax the colonists without giving them representation in Parliament, which is the British lawmaking body.

The French and Indian War was just one part of a worldwide war between Britain and France.

Tea Parties

Although the Stamp Act was **repealed** in 1766, Britain continued to tax the colonies. A very unpopular tax was placed on tea brought into the colonies. On December 16, 1773, a group of patriots in Boston, Massachusetts, dumped British tea into Boston Harbor to protest this tax. The Boston Tea Party, as this event became known, sparked other acts of protest in the colonies, which also became known as "tea parties."

One of the most famous tea parties was held by Penelope Barker of North Carolina on October 25, 1774. The Edenton Tea Party took place in the Edenton, North Carolina, home of Elizabeth King, but it was organized by Barker. She wanted to prove that women could also stand up to the British government. Barker and 50 other women signed a statement of protest, which stated that they would boycott, or stop buying and using, tea and other British goods. While the protest statement was mocked in Britain, it inspired other women in the colonies to boycott British goods.

EDENTON TEA PARTY

Fifty-one women met at Mrs. Elizabeth King's home and resolved, Oct. 25, 1774, to support the American cause.

DIVISION OF ARCHIVES AND HISTORY   1940

The men who participated in the Boston Tea Party wore **disguises** to hide who they were. However, the women who participated in the Edenton Tea Party wanted to prove they were unafraid to show the British who they really were, so they signed their real names to the protest statement.

Boston Tea Party

Fighting the British

The colonies knew they had to stand united against what they felt was unfair treatment by the British. In September 1774, colonial representatives met in Philadelphia, Pennsylvania, to come up with a way to fight Britain's unfair taxes and laws. This became known as the First Continental Congress. William Hooper, Joseph Hewes, and Richard Caswell represented North Carolina at this gathering.

The **tensions** between Britain and the colonies continued to rise until war broke out on April 19, 1775, at Lexington and Concord in Massachusetts. The American Revolution had officially begun.

Patriots throughout North Carolina were prepared to join the American Revolution. In May 1775, it's believed that citizens of the western part of North Carolina gathered in Charlotte to pass the Mecklenburg Resolves, which stated that the Continental Congress was the only governing power in the colonies, not leaders from Britain. That same month, North Carolinian patriots forced their royal governor, Josiah Martin, to leave his official home, Tryon Palace. The patriots in the colony formed their own government, which was known as the North Carolina Provincial Congress.

The First Continental Congress met at Carpenters' Hall in Philadelphia.

A Call to Independence

During the American Revolution, some among the colonists—including some in North Carolina—still supported the British government. These colonists were called loyalists. On February 27, 1776, patriots and loyalists fought in the Battle of Moores Creek Bridge in North Carolina. The patriots won the battle, and it was their first victory in the war.

After the Battle of Moores Creek Bridge, many patriot leaders in North Carolina began to push for independence. On April 12, 1776, members of the North Carolina Provincial Congress met in Halifax and adopted what became known as the Halifax Resolves. The Resolves called for independence from Britain. Later that year, representatives from North Carolina presented the Resolves at a meeting of the Second Continental Congress. North Carolina became the first colonial government to call for total independence from British rule.

The Resolves played a major part in the creation and signing of the Declaration of Independence. This document stated the reasons why the colonies were breaking away from Britain. It was accepted by the Second Continental Congress on July 4, 1776.

The date on the bottom of the North Carolina flag—April 12, 1776—is the date the Halifax Resolves were adopted.

Statehood for North Carolina

During the American Revolution, Britain controlled North Carolina and South Carolina for a time. However, the March 1781 Battle of Guilford Courthouse in North Carolina caused the British to abandon their control over both **colony-states**. Britain won the battle, but they lost many more soldiers than the Americans. This made it easier for the Americans to win at Yorktown, Virginia, in October 1781. That victory ultimately led to Britain's **surrender**.

The war officially ended in 1783. Four years later, a convention was held to improve the new nation's government. However, the convention ended up creating an entirely new Constitution, which is why it's now known as the Constitutional Convention. North Carolina's representatives—William Blount, William Richardson Davie, Alexander Martin, Richard Dobbs Spaight Sr., and Hugh Williamson—didn't want to sign the Constitution without a Bill of Rights, which was proposed in 1789. North Carolina became the 12th state when it **ratified** the Constitution on November 21, 1789.

Glossary

ally: One of two or more people or groups who work together.

clergy: People who are the leaders of a religion and who perform religious services.

colony-state: A term for the American colonies when they were no longer colonies under Britain's rule, but not yet truly free and independent states.

deputy: A second-in-command to a leader.

disguise: Clothes or other things you wear so people will not recognize you.

dispute: An arguement.

enforcement: The act of making sure people do what is required by a law or a rule.

imprison: To put in prison.

permanently: In a lasting manner.

persecution: The act of being treated cruelly or unfairly, especially because of race or religious or political beliefs.

ratify: To formally approve.

repeal: To do away with.

surrender: To agree to stop fighting because you know you will not win or succeed.

tension: A state in which two people, groups, or countries disagree with and feel anger toward each other.

Index

A
American Revolution, 18, 20, 22

B
Battle of Alamance, 13
Battle of Guilford Courthouse, 22
Battle of Moores Creek Bridge, 20
Blackbeard, 11
Boston Tea Party, 16, 17

C
Charles II, 6, 7
Constitutional Convention, 22
Continental Congress, 18, 19, 20
Culpeper's Rebellion, 8, 9

D
Declaration of Independence, 20

E
Edenton Tea Party, 16, 17

F
French and Indian War, 14, 15
Fundamental Constitutions of Carolina, 8

H
Halifax Resolves, 20, 21

L
Lost Colony, 4, 5, 6

M
Mecklenburg Resolves, 18

N
Native Americans, 4, 14
North Carolina Provincial Congress, 18, 20

P
proprietary colony, 6, 7

Q
Quakers, 6, 7

R
Raleigh, Walter, 4, 5
Regulators, 13
royal colony, 12

S
Sons of Liberty, 14
Stamp Act, 14, 16

T
Tryon Palace, 10, 18
Tuscarora War, 11

V
Verrazano, Giovanni da, 4

W
War of Regulation, 13

Primary Source List

p. 4 *Sir Walter Raleigh*. Creator unknown. Oil on panel. 1588. Now kept at the National Portrait Gallery, London, UK.

p. 5 (main) *Arrival of the English*. Created by Theodor de Bry. 1590. Original image included in the book *A Briefe and True Report of the New Found Land of Virginia*, written by Thomas Hariot.

p. 6 Portrait of Charles II. Created by studio of John Riley. Oil on canvas. Ca. 1680 to 1685.

p. 7 *A Quaker Meeting*. Created by Egbert van Heemskerk the Elder or his studio. Oil on canvas. 17th century.

pp. 8–9 Map of Carolina, Virginia, Maryland and New Jersey. Created by J. B. Homann. Ca. 1715. Original image included in Homann's *Atlas Novus*.

Websites

Due to the changing nature of Internet links, PowerKids Press has developed an online list of websites related to the subject of this book. This site is updated regularly. Please use this link to access the list: www.powerkidslinks.com/s13c/nc